SUPERMAN
Doesn't Live Here Anymore

SUPERMAN Doesn't Live Here Anymore

Drugs Are a Lie, Jesus Is the Truth

by Scott McPhillips

Mac on the Attack for Jesus
Honey Creek, IA

© 1998 Scott McPhillips. Printed and bound in the United States of America. All rights reserved. No part of this book may be reproduced or transmitted in any form or by any means, electronic or mechanical, including photocopying, recording, or by an information storage and retrieval system—except by a reviewer who may quote brief passages in a review to be printed in a magazine or newspaper—without permission in writing from the publisher. For information, please contact Mac on the Attack for Jesus, 28535 Coldwater Avenue, Honey Creek, IA 51542.

Although the author and publisher have made every effort to ensure the accuracy and completeness of information contained in this book, we assume no responsibility for errors, inaccuracies, omissions, or any inconsistency herein. Any slights of people, places, or organizations are unintentional.

First printing 1998

ISBN 0-9662205-4-4 (Hardcover)
ISBN 0-9662205-7-9 (Softcover)

LCCN 98-65353

ATTENTION SPORTS ORGANIZATIONS, CORPORATIONS, UNIVERSITIES, COLLEGES, AND PROFESSIONAL ORGANIZATIONS: Quantity discounts are available on bulk purchases of this book for educational purposes. Special books or book excerpts can also be created to fit specific needs. For information, please contact Mac on the Attack for Jesus, 28535 Coldwater Avenue, Honey Creek, IA 51542, phone (712) 545-3003.

CONTENTS

Foreword: *Special K* by Gaylord Schelling vii

Acknowledgments ix

Prologue xi

Beginnings 1

Temptation 4

Good Times, Bad Times 6

The Big Sleep 11

The Awakening 15

On the Rebound 22

Transition 27

Interlude: Reflections and a New Outlook 34

Discovery 40

Afterword: Scott McPhillips
From the Eyes of Others 49

Speech: *On the Rebound* written by
Bill Henjium for Scott McPhillips 58

Where to now, St. Peter?
If it's true, I'm in your hands.
I may not be a Christian,
But I've done all one man can.

I understand I'm on the road
Where all that was is gone,
So where to now, St. Peter?
Show me which road I'm on,
Which road I'm on.

—Bernie Taupin, *Where to Now, St. Peter?*
Knopf Publishing, 1976

FOREWORD

Special K
by Gaylord Schelling

WRITTEN JULY 1991

Gaylord Schelling is the high school football coach in Atlantic, Iowa. Before he moved to Atlantic, Gaylord coached Scott at Tri-Center High School in Neola, Iowa. Coach Schelling's admiration for Scott grew into a friendship that continues today.

A few years ago, Coach Schelling attended a writer's workshop. There, he was challenged by various assignments designed to sharpen his written communication skills. One of those assignments motivated him to write about Scott. The following piece outlines Scott's story, which is an affirmation of the value of life itself and the strength of human will.

■ ■ ■ ■ ■

Scott Krumwiede (who now goes by the name Scott McPhillips) was the best athlete I have ever coached. He was an all-state player in football, basketball, and baseball. He was not, however, the stereotypical all-star athlete. Many athletes shy away from pressure plays, but Scott thrived on them. He loved having the ball during crucial game situations. Scott was a leader both emotionally and physically. He worked very hard in practice and did whatever it took to become great. Probably his best quality was that he never quit, no matter what the score was. Scott amazed me with his ability to come through with the play to win the game.

Like all great people, he had faults. Scott had trouble with drinking and other drugs. We fought and argued over his alcohol abuse. I threatened him and became very frustrated with his lack of self-discipline in this area of his life. Still, no matter how hard I tried, I couldn't get my point about drug abuse through to him.

During Scott's freshman year in college, he had his first automobile accident involving alcohol. He suffered a broken arm and some facial lacerations. After the accident, Scott came to speak to one of my seventh grade classes. He meant well, but he couldn't turn the corner with his alcohol problem. He dropped out of Simpson College, even though he had a good start on his college athletic career. He had started at free safety in football and had pitched some varsity baseball.

A year and a half later, Scott was thinking about going back to Simpson. His mother was looking forward to his return to college.

Then in October 1989, he hit another car head on. The driver of the other car was killed. Scott was trapped in his car for two and a half hours before he was found. He was in surgery for ten hours and suffered unbelievable injuries to all parts of his body except for vital internal organs.

A year and a half later, Scott had undergone numerous surgeries on his arms and legs. This past weekend, he walked into my house for the first time without the aid of a wheelchair or support. Scott still does not remember his great athletic accomplishments, but he has not lost his ability to fight. Few doctors thought he would live, let alone walk and recover the use of his arms or legs. He had to relearn how to speak. Scott's will to "never say never" is his strength.

Now Scott wants to tell his story. He knows he had a problem. He knows he will never be what he once was. It has been a struggle for Scott to learn about life the hard way. He realizes he still has a big battle ahead. Scott has learned a lot, and he wants to let kids know what he has learned and to share the miracle of his recovery. He would like kids to realize there are ways to cope when the struggles of life seem too great without abusing alcohol and drugs.

Life has a purpose; believe it!

ACKNOWLEDGMENTS

I owe so much thanks to so many people, it would take a book at least this big to list them all and what they've done for me.

Always hovering in the background since I was born: Grandmother and Grandfather. They've always been up front when I needed love and support, and have been with me either physically or spiritually all the time. I love both of you very much.

My special thanks to my good friend and mentor, Bob Darrah, whose guidance and encouragement are priceless. A smart man with an abundance of ideas, he always made time to help me grow. He's a great planner and has shown me how to get things done. His confidence in me gives me strength.

Thanks to Bill Henjum, my speech coach. Bill worked with me every weekday for about five months, while this book was being written, to help me speak more clearly to individuals and to groups.

Thanks, too, to my new friend, George Kaywood, whose way with words has helped me to tell my story just the way I want it to be told. He became my confidant during the writing of this book, and I very much appreciate his trust. He made sure every detail was accurate and easy to understand.

Thanks to my mother, Beverly Krumwiede, for her abundant love and endless faith in me (a mother is a special friend); my brother, Steve McPhillips (we had our differences, but I love you); and to Gaylord Schelling, for his direction and support and for being the best coach I ever had.

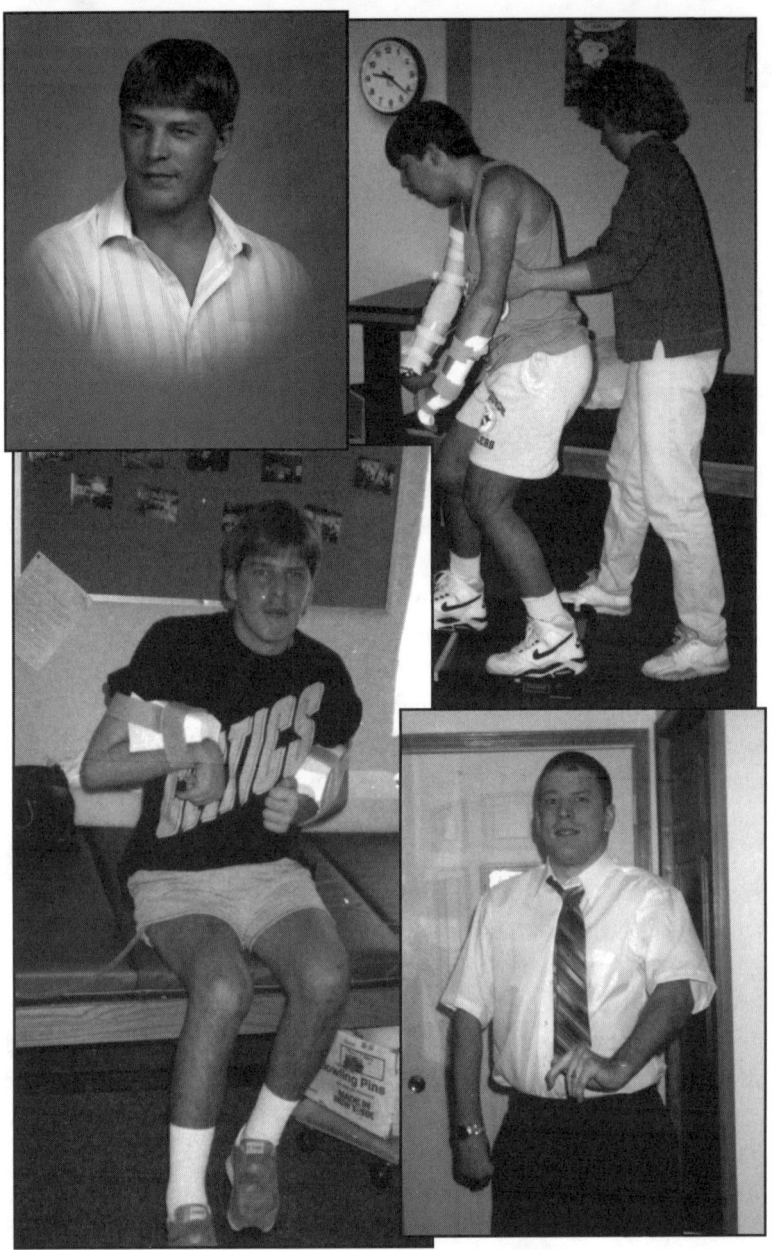

Top left: Just before the accident. **Top right:** 16 months after the accident. Getting closer to walking on my own. **Bottom left:** 8 months after the accident. Finally able to sit up by myself. **Bottom right:** It's Mac on the Attack for Jesus. The new man.

PROLOGUE

It was October 10 when my world changed forever and my life came to a temporary halt. I was on a gravel road in rural Iowa. Drunk and high on drugs, I was driving fast and loose when I approached the crest of a hill. I crashed head on into another car, killing its driver who was also my brother's best friend, Robert Thomas. He was twenty-four years old.

I wish I could describe the accident in great detail and use vivid, graphic descriptions to unsettle you. But I can't because I just don't remember.

It was 1989 when I had the accident. It was 1990 when I woke up. Nine months of my life had vanished. What is nine months? It may not seem like a very long time, but when you're barely out of your teens, it's something akin to forever. Nine months is almost an entire year of school. It's thirty-nine weekends. I missed Thanksgiving. Christmas. New Year's Day. Easter. The Fourth of July. My twenty-first birthday. My life came to a screeching halt, never to be the same again.

Beginnings

My mother says I've been giving people grief ever since the day I was born. I've been strong-willed and impatient all my life, beginning with my entrance into the world during the first winter storm of the season in November 1968. Mom barely made it to the hospital to deliver me.

I grew into a stubborn boy prone to temper tantrums. One of my earliest memories was when I was in second grade and put into "jail." Jail meant I had to leave the classroom and could not come back until I was given permission. After I left the building (with my teacher keeping a close eye on me), I peeked into the classroom window. The other students had been prompted to jeer, and they yelled, "Get away, jailbird! No peeking!" I played on the playground swings for a while but soon grew tired of my unstructured freedom. I quietly snuck back into the school, found a comfortable spot on the floor of the library, and went to sleep. The teacher became alarmed when I vanished from her sight. After a brief search, I was discovered. That was pretty much the end of it, but it was the first of many incidents where Mom was proven right about my ability to give everyone grief.

Frequently, I announced I was running away from home. Mom would say, "Okay," and pack some food. She also made sure I wore something that could be easily spotted, such as a red or orange jacket. Obviously, this type of response makes the decision to run worthless as an attention-getting tactic. I would leave, walk a bit, go behind a tree, then turn around and check to see if anyone was following. Of course, I always went back home. But I did this over and over until it finally dawned on me that it just wasn't any good.

For as long as I can remember, I've been interested in sports. Like many young boys, I wanted to be a professional athlete. The inspiration to excel at sports

When not pitching, I was catching. PeeWee Baseball. Coach Jay Anderson.

was fueled by my brother Steve's success. He was an outstanding quarterback at Neola Tri- Center High School in Iowa before he graduated in 1983. But as much as I admired him, I always wanted to be better than him. And I was.

Most people work hard at developing athletic ability, and some are fortunate enough to be born with a natural predisposition to excel at sports. I was one of the latter types. When I was as young as twelve or thirteen, I played ball with older kids because I was good. I remember enjoying this acceptance by my "elders" and wishing I was older. I practiced to make sure my ball-playing ability would keep me in the company of "the big kids."

Children who have this natural athletic ability are both blessed and cursed. When kids as young as seventh or eighth grade play team sports in school, their coaches try to instill in them the spirit of teamwork. And when one of those students displays superior ability, a coach will always let that student know he or she is better than the rest. This message is sometimes subtle but can never be completely hidden from the rest of the team. The manner of speaking between a coach and the star player sometimes takes on a much different manner than talks to the entire team. I know this because I lived it. As a result, I developed quite an ego at an early age.

When I was out on the playing field, however, I was always willing to do whatever was necessary to help my teammates and coaches. I was a bruiser, but I was a team player. I loved playing football. Sports was my life. Between football seasons, I spent my time playing basketball and baseball. My confidence and pride both skyrocketed when I was named all-state in all three sports.

In high school, sports proficiency is often equivalent to social status or popularity. Students, teachers, family, and townspeople all fed my ego day in and day out. I had a seemingly endless supply of affection and admiration. I was a well-liked, mighty figure who brought recognition and standing to his school and community.

I was a good student who had bad habits. When I think back, I am amazed I was able to make the honor roll. I skipped a lot of school because I was too tired or too hung over. I enjoyed only a few subjects. Because I found these interesting, I paid attention in class and was able to skate through without even taking notes. I passed those courses by being able to recall just enough information for exams, probably in much the same way people who are passionate about certain interests are able to remember almost everything they learn about what they love. Friends did my homework for me in the courses I didn't like. Girls especially were eager to impress me, and I took advantage of them. Some were always willing to keep class notes for me or prep me for exams. I thought I was so smart. I thought I knew everything.

Yes, I had it all. Fame. Success. Love. An easy lifestyle. Hopes for a fabulous future. But I wanted even more. I was being consumed by a lust that would soon start me to lead another kind of life. A life that would almost kill me.

Temptation

I can't remember exactly how or when I began using drugs, but it was some time in junior high school. No one had to coerce me into trying dope. I was Big Man on Campus, but I wanted to be even more cool and more popular. I wanted to experience everything that looked fun and exciting. Thanks to my popularity in school, I was given drugs for free by so-called friends who wanted to hang around with me. I liked the high I got from marijuana. I thought I could handle it.

My life soon revolved around sports, women, alcohol, and drugs, usually in that order. Booze, grass, pills, coke, acid—I did it all with one exception: I'm happy to say I never stuck a needle into my arm. I've seen others do it, but no matter how high I ever got or wanted to get, if someone offered me a needle, I always refused. I never needed to get off that badly.

Some people were surprised drugs were as accessible in a small Iowa town as in a big city. The situation was wide open during the eighties. If you wanted it, you could get it. At first, transactions were done away from school, but once you proved you were skillful enough to buy, store, and use drugs cleverly enough so no one suspected anything, deals went down on the school grounds as well.

In junior high, I only did drugs at night, away from school property and away from home. I was able to conceal my drug use from everyone, including my family. I made up excuses as to my whereabouts. I would say I was "going out with friends," "going on a date," or some other reason that never aroused suspicion. Because I got away with it, my ego was fed even more. I was successful at everything I wanted to do. The cocky little boy was king.

During my high school years, I became a heavy drug user. I did drugs every morning, every night, and whenever else I could. The more I took, the more I wanted to reach a higher high. My state of mind was "gimme, gimme, gimme!"

I remember going into my world geography class every day higher than a kite because I did drugs before class. I remember playing in a football game with a vial of cocaine in my hip pocket. I thought using coke would improve my game. It never dawned on me that some of my best games were played without drugs.

Soon, the drugs I got for free were not enough, and I became a regular buyer when freebies weren't available. It was just the cost of having fun. I worked my way into the network of people who bought and sold drugs. I became a small-time dealer—not to make money but to earn enough cash to cover my own habit. I was able to support my own desires comfortably thanks to the number of willing buyers I met in school.

I may have fooled my family, but I wasn't able to fool my friends. My own inner circle of friends (real friends, not the ones who did drugs with me and saw nothing wrong with it) could see I was into drugs and tried to stop me. They didn't preach but they made it clear they wanted me to stop. They tried many times to convince me I was hurting myself. No one, including the girls who were doing my homework and trying to impress me, could make me listen. I thought—and said—"Get away from me! I'm on top of the world!"

And on top of the world I stayed, becoming more and more confident I would never fall. I had everything I wanted in life, and it looked like there was even more to come.

Good Times, Bad Times

Mr. Tough Guy (Maniac).

Knowing you're good and not letting it go to your head is one of the most difficult things in the world for anyone—especially a kid—to master. Sure, there were hours of practice, drills, pep talks, all the things that big school athletes need to become winners. For me it was not work but a lot of fun.

My school (Tri-Center High School) went to the state level of competition in football, basketball, and baseball for the 1985–1986 school year. We placed second in both basketball and baseball—not bad for a small school in a small Iowa farm town. The following year, I was selected as an all-state athlete in all three

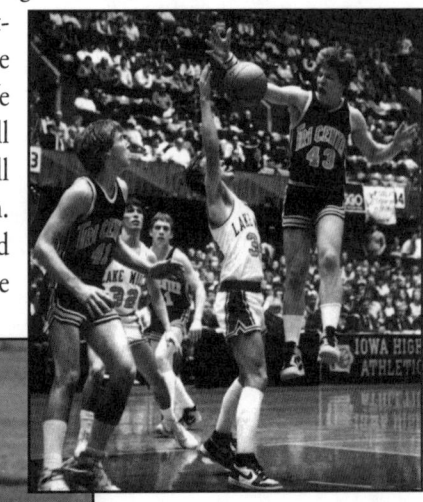

Sky high for the ball.

Ready to hurl a 94 mph fast ball.

sports. My goal of becoming a professional athlete seemed to be getting closer.

Tri-Center captured the Iowa State Baseball Championship in 1987. I pitched a good game and even hit a home run the first time I came to bat. I was also named the game's most valuable player. Or so I've been told. Because of my accident, I cannot remember the greatest accomplishments of my sports career.

Being interviewed by press after winning the state championship.

In fall 1987, I was eighteen years old and just starting to trade adolescence for adulthood. I enrolled in Simpson College in Indianola, Iowa. Simpson was only a couple of hours away from home, but far enough away from any restrictions you have to observe when living with your family. When I made the move from Honey Creek to Indianola, drugs moved with me. I quickly learned how to contact the "right" people and found they were like everyone else I'd met in high school: It was a big deal for them to supply and do drugs with the star athlete.

Life at the men-only dorm Barker Hall was one big party. My sports skills cemented my image as Big Man on Campus. I had four different girlfriends vying for my affection. I kept my grades just strong enough to stay out of academic trouble. And the drug pipeline was open and working.

Then on Wednesday night, October 22, 1987, a friend and I were headed east on Interstate 80, returning to Indianola after partying in Des Moines. We were both high, driving fast in my brother's new black sports car, which I had borrowed for a few days. No one knows how the accident happened. All that is definite is that the car hit a guardrail. I must have thought I was in trouble because the first thing I did when I heard the wail of police sirens was to run. I'm told I ran

What's left of the car.

across the interstate, put my broken arm on a fencepost, jumped over the fence, and hollered back at my friend, "Good-bye! See ya tomorrow!"

I have a hazy memory of running along a set of railroad tracks, falling on some cinders, and seeing a broken bone sticking out of my arm. The police radioed for a medical helicopter, and it's a good thing they did. The searchlight on the helicopter spotted me lying on the ground after I had passed out. The last thing I remember is being helped by some policemen. Then darkness.

The luck that seemed to be a natural part of my life was still with me. Whoever witnessed or came upon the accident must have reported it quickly. I was pretty banged up, and if there had been much of a delay, I might not have lived. I was rushed to the hospital in Des Moines. After it was determined how much surgery I would need for my injuries, one of the two specialists who would have to operate on me coincidentally happened to be in Des Moines at the time.

My left forearm was fractured. Compound. The doctors had to fit a steel plate on what was left to hold it together. It's still there today. Unless you touched my arm, you'd never known how mangled it was. Of course, you don't want to touch my arm, because the feel of steel under live skin is so unusual, it's enough to spook just about anybody.

My face was cracked open when it hit the steering wheel, requiring seventy-two stitches on the outside and another seventy-two stitches on the inside. The stitches

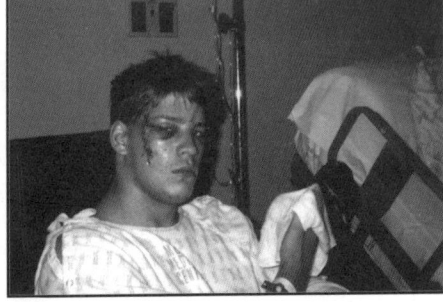

Pretty boy?

ran from my right eye halfway down to my chin. Again, I was lucky—my face healed without producing any ugly scars, but I've still got a couple of permanent hash marks to remind me of that night every time I look into a mirror. And believe it or not, the only thing I was worried about at the time was if the girls would still be attracted to me in spite of an ugly scar on my face! I told myself the scar would make me look tougher, more macho, so maybe it wasn't that bad after all.

I have no doubt today this accident was a warning from God. He was trying to show me what my real friends had been trying to tell me: I was throwing my life away and headed for serious trouble if I kept living a drug-based lifestyle. Had I heeded God's warning, the big fall that followed might never have happened.

I didn't listen. My ego continued to get stroked. When I was in high school, I made sports headlines regularly and thrived on it. Kevin White, a writer for *The Daily Nonpareil* in Council Bluffs, Iowa, wrote these words during my rehabilitation. At the time, I felt it was one of the highest compliments I ever received.

Going up for two.

...And this is a guy who was not your everyday athlete. He was flat gifted. People said he couldn't play the post position in basketball at 5-foot-10. But his senior year, he was simply unstoppable, averaging 25.7 points and 11.3 rebounds a game. The scoring average was easily the best ever for one season at Tri-Center. He also ended up as the sixth best rebounder in T-C [Tri-Center High School] history.

Whatever he lacked in height, he more than made up for in pure effort. When you got in a game he'd find a way to beat you.

...(Scott was)...unquestionably one of the best athletes the school has ever produced.

■ ■ ■ ■ ■

I healed quickly. But my playing days on the football field were over. It would be impossible for me to play football with a steel plate in my arm. My doctor added that with the head injury I had sustained, one good hit or body slam and...well, it's not a pretty picture.

In addition to the depressing realization I could never play football again, I couldn't swing a baseball bat very well because of the injuries to my arm. My baseball career was on hold indefinitely. In addition, I didn't like my baseball coach, John Siriani, because he was always on my back to study and improve my grades. Now I realize he was right, I was wrong, and he has become a friend. I quickly lost interest in Simpson College and decided I had no reason to stay in Indianola. I dropped out of Simpson and returned home with plans to enroll in Iowa Western Community College in nearby Council Bluffs. Iowa Western had a pretty good baseball team, and I thought I could play baseball once I got there.

I started classes during the 1988–1989 term, but true to form, I concentrated on fun and games rather than getting a degree. I don't remember much of the time I spent there, but I failed every class. I managed to play a little baseball there but did nothing noteworthy. The assistant coach, Kevin Whitehall, said I was a good person but had some bad habits. What an understatement! I still couldn't see how much success and opportunity I had thrown away or how I was continuing to destroy my life.

The Big Sleep

After an accident as damaging as the first one I had, it's amazing I didn't change my lifestyle. I should have gotten the message I'd better change my ways to make sure something like that would never happen again. But even after the pain of my corrective surgery, the awful realization I couldn't play football anymore, and the awareness that my chances of becoming a professional athlete were slim or none, it was still party time.

That is, until that fateful night in October 1989, when my world came crashing down around me, and I fell off the top of the world.

While I was in that nine-month coma my sports career came to an end. My education stopped. My prestige and popularity faded away. My girlfriends, concerned at first, drifted away. My friends grew distant. My growth as a human being was put on hold. "Out of sight, out of mind" is true. Time pushes things away—people, pain, emotions, even values. During my nine months of being out of sight, literally and figuratively, my entire life changed. I can only blame myself. I lived carelessly. I let my ego dictate my actions, never for a moment considering the consequences.

I don't remember anything during that period of time. I thank God for the faith and courage of my mother, Beverly Krumwiede. Fortunately, she had the presence of mind and the strength to write down what happened and her thoughts and the decisions she had to make for me. Here's what she wrote:

■ ■ ■ ■ ■

It began for me with a phone call at one in the morning. "Your son is being life-flighted to St. Joseph's Hospital in Omaha. I suggest you get there as soon as possible."

After I reached the hospital, I rushed into the emergency room. There were so many doctors and nurses surrounding Scott that I couldn't even see him. They let me talk to him at 3:00 A.M., as they were wheeling him to surgery. They thought he might be able to hear me.

Scott required many operations. The doctors were extremely nice and caring, as they came out between each round of surgery, explaining what they had done and were going to do next. For example: (1) placed a rod in the left femur, which had been broken in four or five places; (2) fixed the right knee; (3) put in an external pelvic apparatus to correct the pelvic bones that had been pulled four inches apart, causing a small puncture in the bladder; and (4) put screws in the right foot to fix the broken talus bone.

The surgery ended at 1:00 P.M. the next afternoon. It had taken ten hours for the doctors to finish their work. There was a lapse of four hours from the accident itself, which happened at 9:15 P.M., until Scott got to the hospital. He was not found for two and a half hours, and then it took over an hour to get him out of the car.

I was not ready for the shock of seeing Scott in intensive care. A blue wire was attached to his head, actually connected through the scalp to his brain, to monitor brain pressure. A tube protruded up and out of his right lung, which had been punctured and deflated in the accident. His right leg was in a cast. He had a respirator to help him breathe.

Scott developed a fever. 105 degrees. At one point, his breathing suddenly became faster and shallower. Pneumonia in the left lung. Another tube. Another machine.

So many machines. So many "beeps" and screaming-type sounds. At least that's what they sounded like to me. I was petrified whenever a warning signal sounded. Each one triggered the same thought: "My God, he's going to die and no one is running in here to help him!"

After the hospital staff explained what each sound meant, the panic went away. I hope that hospital care personnel everywhere ex-

plain what all the machines are, and what all the sounds mean as soon as possible to parents unfortunate enough to go through what I did. It will help them a lot.

I'll always be thankful for all the information the hospital staff at St. Joseph's gave to me personally. It doesn't matter how much printed information you're given. After an accident like the one Scott was in, you're simply not in a state of mind to comprehend much of what you read.

One bit of advice I'm especially thankful for was, "The more you are with him and can talk to him, the better and faster he will come out of it." I think I'll always be remembered at St. Joseph's as the Mom who read and talked to her son all but the last ten minutes of every two hours in intensive care.

Scott was in intensive care at St. Joseph's for 26 days. He was moved to the rehabilitation section of Immanuel Medical Center in Omaha on December 5, 1989.

In February 1990, I moved Scott to Independence, Missouri, to continue his treatment as an inpatient in a program that specialized in people with head-injuries. At this time, Scott's left arm and hand had too much muscle tone. It had twisted so that if you didn't keep a pillow at his elbow, he could choke himself. His right arm had little or no muscle tone, and was drawn up with his hand dropped. His right leg was drawn up, and his shoulders and body were starting to draw up into a fetal position.

■ ■ ■ ■ ■

I did not learn about Rob's death for a long time after the fatal crash. During my rehabilitation, I was able to go home on weekends. On one of those visits, my mother took me to a baseball game where I saw Rob Thomas's older brother. Unaware Rob had died in the crash, I said something half-jokingly about Rob to him. He looked at me oddly and said, "You don't know what happened," and walked away. I still feel bad about having to wait so long to find out.

Seeing how puzzled I was, Mom asked my psychologist about telling me the truth. He told her she could decide when to tell me based on how she thought I would handle it. She chose to tell me while we were staying in Kansas City one weekend near the complex where I was undergoing rehabilitation. The psychologist would be close by if I needed help. As I lay on the bed in our motel room, she told me that on the night of the accident, my car had not hit a tree as I had been told earlier.

"You met a car head on at the crest of a hill," she said quietly.

"Who was in the other car?" I asked.

"Rob Thomas."

"How is Rob?" I asked with a sense of foreboding.

"Rob is in heaven with God." She looked at me. "God has called Rob home. All of our days are numbered, you know."

I didn't know what to say. I couldn't believe it. I lay there in silence, rolling the realization over and over in my mind. What could I possibly have said that would have made any sense after hearing I had killed someone?

I think about Rob's death every day. It's like a knife sticking through my heart. Is there any way to ever put aside the knowledge you caused another person to lose his life because of your own stupidity?

There are times today when I find it hard to believe I've actually been through all this. I don't feel sorry for myself, however, because I know it's all part of God's plan for me. It's a terribly hard way to learn a simple lesson, but had it not been for the accident, I probably would never have learned what's really important in life.

The Awakening

Just what is a coma?

The dictionary defines it as "a state of deep unconsciousness, caused by disease, injury, or poison." But this is not necessarily accurate. Most people think you're either in a coma or not in a coma—completely unconscious or completely awake. According to Dr. Gene Rankin, a neuropsychologist at Immanuel Medical Center in Omaha, Nebraska, there are various degrees of comas. One type (usually represented in the movies) is deep and extreme. People in this type of coma do not respond to or feel pain. People in a near-coma seem to be awake but are unaware of what is going on around you. And there are gradations between those two extremes.

According to medical reports, I went through many different coma stages. While I was at St. Joseph's, I gave no response to questions or to pain. After moving to Immanuel, although I still couldn't talk, I blinked my eyes once or twice in response to "yes" and "no" questions. (Dr. Rankin says eye blink tests, however, are not considered reliable because it's hard to get consistent results. Some say I was consistent. Take your pick.) And in Independence, I continued the eye blinks, started to nod my head, and so on. At least, that's what I'm told.

It wasn't until July 1990 that I really woke up, opened my eyes, and was able to think, "Where am I? What's going on here?" I had been on various medications that were supposed to help me reach this "normal" level of awareness and had very recently had an operation. Sometimes the effect of an operation combined with medications and other conditions can trigger an awakening from a coma. Whatever triggered it, I was "back."

The moment I opened my eyes I knew something was wrong. Fear gripped me. My hands and arms were crossed and I couldn't move them. In fact, I couldn't move much of my body at all having had the unconscious tendency to scrunch up into a fetal position so much. At first I thought I had taken some contaminated drugs. Maybe I was on some crazy type of a bad trip.

Then, a moment or two later, I thought I was at home. I tried to yell out, "Mom!" Alerted by the half-formed sounds I made, the first words anyone had heard me utter in months, two nurses came rushing in.

"Do you know where you are?" one asked.

Confused, I mouthed, "No."

"You're in the hospital, " one nurse told me.

An overdose, I thought to myself. I did too many drugs this time and wound up overdosing.

The nurses' short explanation hit me like a bullet: "You were in an accident and you've been in a coma for nine months."

What's left of my car.

It was impossible to comprehend the full meaning of those few words. I tried to ask questions, as if a survival reflex had been tweaked. I wanted and needed information.

I couldn't talk. I wanted to say, "Where's my mother? I want to talk to Mom," but I must have uttered something like, "Muhhhh?"

"Your mother's not here right now, but she'll be very happy to know you've come out of your coma. She'll be here this weekend."

I tried to ask, "Where's my brother?" I didn't hear the answer. As I listened to my own words, I thought, "My God! My speech is so slurred! I can't believe how bad I sound! I can hardly make a sound!"

One of the nurses asked me, "Do you know what year it is?"

I thought to myself, "Sure. It's 1989."

"It's 1990, Scott."

Nineteen-ninety. My life had stopped before I was able to turn the calendar. I was still in 1989.

Why couldn't I remember what happened? I tried, but I could not recall any details of that terrible night…and I still can't remember to this day. Was my mind blocking out the awful sounds, smells, and pain of my own massive wounds, as well as the death of my brother's best friend? Was it part of the head injury that affected my speech and ability to move? Or, most likely, a little bit of both?

My disbelief at what was happening was pushed aside for the moment by the announcement that I had undergone surgery on my right leg. I tried my best to ask why I had needed the surgery.

"So you'll be able to walk," was the simple explanation.

I thought, "Ridiculous! Me, an all-state sports star, needing surgery to walk. Of course I can walk!"

I wanted to tell them I didn't need a wheelchair. I knew I could walk. I would show them.

But of course I couldn't get up. My nurses smiled at me. They were so happy I had come out of my coma after nine months that my "cocky little boy" attitude made no difference.

It's always a big deal—often rightfully called a miracle—when someone comes out of a coma. Soon after I awoke, doctors and nurses hurried into and out of the room, or so it seemed to me. Although they quickly told me where I was and how I had arrived there, I had a very difficult time trying to understand what my mind was doing in this really screwed-up body.

Soon after the uproar died down, I learned I was at Rebound, a unit of the Independence Regional Health Center in Independence, Missouri. Rebound specialized in patients with head injuries who needed extensive therapy both physically and mentally if they were to lead what most people would call normal lives. Mom had decided it would be the best place for me. (I use the past tense in describing Rebound, because after I left, HealthSouth Rehabilitation Corporation bought the center and Rebound is officially known today as the Kansas City Rehabilitation Network.)

I am indebted to the people at Rebound. They are responsible for my rebirth.

My life at Rebound was a combination of introspection, physical and mental exercise, discovery, and learning. Rehabilitation at Rebound was divided into two parts: first, time spent as an in-patient; later, living by yourself on the grounds as part of the transition back to life outside an environment of structured care. Not only did I need different types of therapy to regain the ability to walk, reason, and simply use my body the way most people take for granted, I had to relearn many simple tasks ranging from bathroom habits to dressing myself.

When I began my stay as an in-patient at Rebound, someone told me what the day and date were before I went to sleep every night. When I got up the next morning, I could not remember either. Occasionally, I would even forget where my room was.

For a long part of my stay at Rebound as an in-patient, someone had to dress me every morning—and change my diapers! I had to wear them because I could not communicate to anyone when I had to use the toilet. I didn't have any control of my bladder at that time because my brain was not sending messages to my body for various functions that require your mind and body to work together. And when you gotta go, you gotta go. It was incredibly degrading to be aware of what was happening but having no control over it.

For about two years, I had to wear special brace-like devices when I went to bed at night. I became very frustrated when I had to wait for help to get into and out of bed every day. In the hospital, you have to learn to wait your turn, but the need to have someone always helping you aggravates even slight discomforts.

If you can, think back to when you were a small child. Do you remember how many times you tried to get a button through a buttonhole? Trying over and over again to tie your shoes? If that takes you too far back, then think about when you first learned to ride a bicycle. How many times did you wobble, fall off, get up, and do it again before you learned what the proper balance should feel like?

That's what it was like for me, except I already knew what should happen, how the simple routines of daily life worked and how they should feel. But I couldn't do them. I had to learn like a child does. The learning process was repetitive, slow, and very frustrating.

The person who did the most for me was Mom. She made the 222-mile trip from her house to Rebound every weekend to pick me up so I could be home with family and friends. She would pick me up at Rebound, take me home for a couple of days, then take me back to Rebound on Sunday night. That's 888 miles every weekend!

These weekly road trips became as much a part of my therapy

Above: Home with my pets. Trying to make my arms move to pet the cat.

Right: Home after first surgery with friend. Biggest smile I could get. Notice my hands.

as the more formal routines at Rebound. I discovered I could talk to Mom about anything. If I ever got out of line, she'd let me know about it. If she said I was wrong about something, I later realized I was really wrong. The practice of talking about and listening to ideas and the events that had happened in my life helped to shape the values I have today. I'm sure it was tiring for her, but it was an important part of rebuilding my life.

Mom continued to keep a journal, and the notes she made while I was at Rebound tell some stories worth sharing. Here's part of her journal from that time:

■ ■ ■ ■ ■

The first weekend I drove to Independence to see Scott, I was very upset to see him sitting in a wheelchair with a padded board behind his back for support. He had to be strapped in, with straps over his shoulders to hold him up. The therapists explained to me, "When you put yourself at a sharp 90-degree angle, what do you feel? It's a message to your brain. Relax and put yourself in a reclining position, and what do you feel? Nothing."

I remember watching Rebound staff members struggling with Scott just to get him from his bed to a chair. His feet always hit the floor. They said to me, "Stomp your feet on the floor. What do you feel? It's a message to your brain!" They were trying to get Scott's brain to receive messages and make his body respond to them.

Every weekend, there was some little bit of improvement: Scott's nodding his head "yes," shaking it side to side for "no," shrugging his shoulders, moving the wheelchair backwards, and later pulling it forward, first with both feet and eventually with one foot after

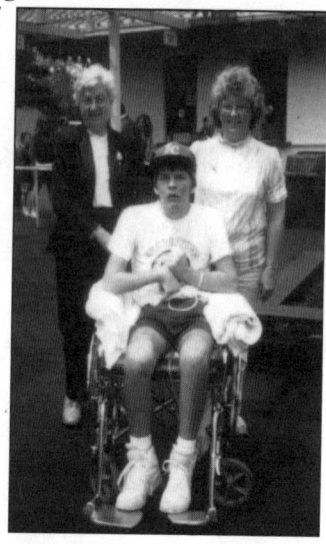

Mother's Day 1990. Grandma, Mom and Scott at Worlds of Fun.

the other. I remember him trying to talk. He communicated by shaking his head "yes" or "no" in response to someone pointing to letters on a clipboard, spelling out words one letter at a time.

I knew Scott could process thoughts. One proof of this came from this exercise: Scott would sit on the edge of the bed with Grandma supporting him. He would put his feet on my legs as I sat on the floor. I would ask him a simple arithmetic problem, and he would tap out the answer on my legs with one of his feet!

During a visit one weekend, we took a shopping trip to a mall not too far from Rebound. It looked like Scott was starting to do much better. He tried on fifty pairs of sunglasses until he found just the right one. (It had Budweiser printed on it. I persuaded him to take his second choice.) Next, he chose a pair of tennis shoes by himself. He went to the pet shop twice to play with the dogs and even ate some candy I shouldn't have given him. The trip back to Rebound took just fifteen minutes. When Scott went inside and the nurses asked him where he had gone, he just shrugged his shoulders. He couldn't remember.

Our faith in God was our strength to help us through difficult times. I knew Scott could hear me before he could move. Before I left him at night, I would say the Lord's Prayer. After saying "Amen," he would breathe a deep, contented sigh. Many people who work for the same company as I, prayed for Scott, including some as far away as Canada, Germany, South Africa, and Brazil.

I visited Scott every weekend. We would go to church on Sunday. I remember in June of 1990 when I had to bodily lift him from the car to a wheelchair. I was so happy when he was able to walk up and kneel at the alter by himself.

One Monday morning during that same month, as I was driving back to Iowa from Kansas City, the sun was shining through the most beautiful white clouds. I heard a voice say, "He's going to be all right."

I thank God and all who have helped Scott on his road to recovery.

■ ■ ■ ■ ■

On The Rebound

I was surprised rehabilitation and therapy began almost immediately and did not take a backseat to the surgeries that accompanied my program at Rebound. I was so banged up it took fourteen operations before the damage done to my body was repaired as well as it could be.

In July 1990, Dr. Gregory Hummel lengthened my right leg. It was just after this surgery I started to remember things I could not previously recall. Other operations followed: October 1990—left arm lengthened; December 1990—right arm lengthened; February 1991—left hand brought out and fingers pinned out; June 1991—right hand brought out by rerouting a tendon from the bottom side of the wrist to the top side of the hand.

The most painful of all the operations—I wince at the thought even today—was the surgery on my hands. My hands and fingers had to be stretched out from the curled position they assumed during the coma. Nothing ever hurt as badly as that. My occupational therapist, Jane Cox, had to physically prestretch my fingers before surgery, and when she did, I cursed at her and cussed up a storm! I couldn't figure out why she was hurting me so much.

After I had surgery on my left hand, I relearned how to brush my teeth. It wasn't until after the surgery I could open my hand to put a toothbrush in it or turn it to reach my mouth.

Oddly, some of my indulgent attitude and behavior before the accident may have actually helped speed my recovery. Oleatta, the receptionist at Rebound, was single and a fox. I had the hots for her. I always perked up and was on my best behavior when I knew I'd have the chance to talk to her. I was at her desk as much as possible. Kathy Sloan, one of my nurses, was a gorgeous woman and a real inspiration for me to want to get better as fast as I could. I always thought on certain days she wore low-cut blouses, but that perception may have been more wish than reality. Oleatta and Kathy used to give me a little kiss for luck before each operation. In some way, that made me actually look forward to surgery.

I never thought I would have to learn to dress myself again. One of my major accomplishments was putting on my own socks without help. There I was, a grown man, understanding what to do but unable to do it because my brain wouldn't send the proper messages to my hands. It was a humbling experience. The cocky little boy was gone for good.

It was a personal milestone when I could get up from sitting or lying down and go to the bathroom alone. It signified what I hoped would be the first of many major accomplishments. It seems hard to believe something this simple could be so important, but it was. And although it was a long time ago, I've never forgotten how meaningful it was. I've reflected many times on how unexpectedly values can change your life.

For a long time, I had to read material in large print, designed for the visually impaired. Much of this was books designed for very young children—I hated having to read those kiddie books! But, like other parts of my body, the muscles in my eyes had been weakened and had to be built back up. I was very excited when I started to read the newspaper by myself. I still remember the date: January 25, 1992. I was so excited, I called Mom at home to tell her. This meant I would be all right on my own, if and when I returned to school.

One of the most important things that happened during my rehabilitation was realizing I could admit when I was wrong. Remember, I was used to calling all the shots. How ironic. Less than a year before the accident, I expected others to do things for me. Afterward, I needed people to do things for me. Although I was not inconsiderate before the accident, I learned at Rebound how to be more helpful to others. I found myself going out of my way to help people, especially those who were in worse shape than I was.

As I became more able to do things for myself physically, my emotions went through several phases. I went through a stage of anger. I was mad at the world in general. I was mad at myself for having reached the lowest point in my life. I threw what can only be called temper tantrums, lashing out at the people who were trying to help me. It infuriated me whenever someone at Rebound told me, "Be appropriate. Don't swear. Be kind to everybody." Thankfully, this period passed quickly.

Some of the doctors who examined me did not believe I'd ever be able to walk again. Others told me, "It is not going to be easy, but after what we've heard about you, if anyone can do it, you can." I never doubted for a moment, however, that I would walk again. The skepticism of the doctors who thought it was unlikely was offset by the encouragement of family, friends, and doctors who thought it might be possible.

There was much work to do in daily therapy sessions. I became focused on learning to walk again, and it became my number one personal goal at Rebound. It was very frustrating. Because I had walked all of my life before the accident, I knew how to walk. But my brain wouldn't send the signals to my legs to walk. At the very beginning of the therapy specifically designed to help me to walk again, one of the therapists said to me, "So you want to walk on your own? Well, get up and walk!"

I asked for help getting up from the chair I was in. Everyone, including me, was amazed when I took a small step forward with my left leg, alone. But when I went to move my right leg, *whomp!* They caught me before I fell flat on the floor. I was unable to use crutches to make learning how to walk easier. Because of my head injury, my arms were affected such that it was impossible for me to place crutches under them. It was either tough it out or not at all. But I never faltered in my belief that I would walk again.

Dance therapy may sound like a strange way to begin to teach someone to walk again, but it's really quite logical. Your dance "partner," a physical therapist, uses her arms to help you keep your balance, training those atrophied and unused muscles to feel what it's like to be working again. She helps keep you up in case you start to fall. And she decides how much is enough per session, so you're not fatigued and your muscles are not overly taxed. The rhythm of music also helps to act as a guide for simple movement. You might say it's the grandaddy of aerobic dancing.

I also used to practice just walking. It actually took a total of four people to get me walking when I took those first steps: One person had to hold up my butt, another held the rest of my body upright, a third shuffled my legs to create a walking rhythm, and a fourth person stood by in case any extra help was needed. Randy Leighton, a physical therapist, would put his arm around my waist for support or hold my hips up until the muscles were strong enough to support me without help. He also helped me walk up and down stairs without using a handrail. We started with just half a flight of steps at a time and progressed to four full flights. I went up and down those four flights of stairs every day for a long time. The therapists cautioned me not to overdo it, but I've always been an overachiever and I pushed myself as hard as I could every time I exercised. Randy knew how important it was to me to be able to walk again, and he helped me a great deal.

Cindy helping me to walk steps.

I knew my legs (which had also been injured) would have to be strengthened considerably before I'd ever be able to walk again. Thanks to my sports background, I knew one way to do this. I worked with the therapists to develop a program of sit-ups. Once I started, I was not content to do sets of twenty-five, fifty, or even one hundred at a time. I usually did sets of three hundred. I got to the point where I could do well over a thousand per morning and afternoon session. Yes, it was hard work, but I could feel the muscles developing. I knew by sticking with it, I'd reach the day when I could say, "I can walk," much sooner.

It took over more than a year before I walked on my own again, but I'll never forget the date. It was on May 10, 1991, the high point of my rehabilitation.

All of the therapists and nurses at Rebound were masters of motivation. Cindy Reagan, my physical therapist, was the first therapist to teach me how to walk. I made a game of hiding and making her search for me. Betty Rugh, my night nurse, encouraged me to begin the sit-up program that strengthened my legs. I used to sleep from four o'clock in the afternoon until eight just so I could stay up and talk to her all night. She was my mother's age and gorgeous. (A lot of my old characteristics were coming through!) She was a real inspiration to me. She told me to get off the "pitty pot" and do something constructive like sit-ups.

Therapist Brad Jackson also helped me out. He was a big, strong black man whose sense of humor will stay with me forever. We always called each other "home boy." He is black and I am white, but we realized we both had the same creator. Kevin Birch, an on-call therapist, was like a big brother to me. He lived in one of the apartments at Rebound. I spent a lot of time in his apartment talking about anything and everything. Lee Harrison was my speech therapist. She was the first person to teach me to pronounce sounds and words again. Boy, was she patient! We would go through the alphabet and enunciate individual sounds, all simple things but very important to my recovery.

Kay Williams was my in-patient psychologist and also my second mother. She taught me how to have patience. She got me out of a lot of trouble with the nursing staff. I will always be greatly appreciative for all the troubles she helped get me out of and for helping me to understand.

Toward the end of my stay as an in-patient at Rebound, I got the feeling that the staff was ready for me to move ahead, to do more by myself. Creating this feeling of forward movement was the best thing they could have done for me. I was ready to take more control of my life. But I was not expecting a bigger change would happen—a change that helped to give me direction and purpose for the future.

Transition

TRANSITIONS

The following is the official list of qualifications from Rebound that must be met by patients advancing to the transitional phase of therapy. Note how most items are things people take for granted. It's somewhat unnerving to see them spelled out this way.

(Structured) Apartment Living Admission Criteria
1. Evidence of acquired brain injury (e.g., trauma, surgical, circulatory, anoxia)
2. Eighteen years of age or older
3. Cognitive level VII / VIII
4. Previously underwent some type of head injury rehabilitation therapy
5. Absence of communicable or contagious disease
6. Potential for further rehabilitation
7. Functional mobility
8. Functional communication
9. Ability to plan for future
10. Life Survival Skills
    a. Ability to plan daily activity
    b. Ability to plan and prepare all meals
    c. Ability to be independent in cleaning skills, laundry
    d. Ability to record information
    e. Ability to perform three-step problem solving

     f. Able to access community with assist from Rebound staff
11. Behavioral
     a. Ability to live with roommate
     b. Ability to negotiate
     c. Compliance with daily therapy schedule
     d. Has appropriate social skills
     e. Does not require supervision
     f. Understands rules and complies with them

NOTE: Rebound is now known as the Kansas City Rehabilitation Network. The name was changed after the HealthSouth Rehabilitation Corporation bought Rebound, Inc.

■ ■ ■ ■ ■

The goal of the second part of Rebound's rehabilitation program is to help patients live independently. You are moved from living as an in-patient in a ward-like setting to living pretty much alone. One of the qualifications for advancing into this part is the ability to walk by yourself or to transfer yourself from a wheelchair without help. You live "on campus," but you have your own apartment, similar to a college dormitory. You're on your own, but there's a "safety net" close by if you need it. Once you've relearned the basics to get you through the day, you need to relearn how to live life as well as how to do life.

Rather than being thrilled to move into my own apartment in April 1991, I was angry because the people at Rebound stopped doing things I could now do myself. No one waited on me anymore. I went through an anger stage during the early stages of in-patient rehabilitation, so I guess it wasn't unusual to have to pass through another one as I went through the early stages of transitional rehabilitation.

As an in-patient, you learn simple movements and little things to make your mobility and mind-body coordination stronger. As a transitional patient, you learn more specific skills. I like to think of it as fine-tuning your life.

It was during this transitional phase that I learned how to dress myself again. I remember the staff taking the shoelaces off my shoes and

Left: Learning how to wash my clothes.
Above: Clearing my dishes.

attaching Velcro strips to "tie" the shoes, so I could get them on and off by myself. I learned how to wash my own clothes. I still ate meals in a cafeteria, but now it was up to me to clear my own dishes when I was finished. I joined other transitional patients in the cafeteria kitchen once a week to help prepare the food we ate, with the cooks giving us simple tasks to perform.

Before the accident I always thought of doing laundry, cooking, and cleaning as women's work. In transitional rehabilitation, I felt a sense of accomplishment when I was able to do it all for myself. These things became ordinary facts of life instead of tasks I once used to selfishly manipulate others to do for me.

Dressing myself and going to the bathroom whenever I needed to without help from another person became daily pleasures for me. One of my most enjoyable pastimes was simply watching television and eating popcorn. Think about that for a minute—watching television and having a snack of your own choice. I suppose most people don't give watching television and having a snack a second thought. But suppose you were disabled so that:

You can't sit in a chair without help from someone.

You can't communicate that you want to watch TV or change channels.

You can't get up and move to do it yourself.

You can't adjust the volume to suit your comfort.

You can't prepare a snack because your hands and arms won't do what you want them to.

You can't eat a snack because your arm won't bend so your hand can reach your mouth.

Does that make it easier to understand how excited I was to be able to do something as simple as watch TV and eat popcorn?

Transitional life at Rebound was not without funny moments and fond memories. When you spend a lot of time with people, it's natural to develop friendships and bonds. My best friend at Rebound was a fellow patient named Kenny. He had fallen off the roof of a two-story house, injuring his head. Because of my own injuries, my speech was very poor then and it was difficult to understand what I was saying. Kenny had the same disability, but we could understand each other without any problem! It appeared to others we had a language of our own. We used to drive the nurses in the hospital crazy because we could conduct seemingly normal conversations and the nurses couldn't understand a word we were saying!

Kenny was very bright and a real inspiration to me. He had a positive outlook on everything. Being in a wheelchair didn't bother him a bit. He used to tease the nurses as much as I did. I was very happy when Kenny made it to the transitional phase. I think he was one of the few people there who really understood what I had been through as he and I shared some of the same physical problems.

Some patients in transition had roommates. I did not have one for a long time because of my preference for keeping the room temperature cool. Well, I called it cool; to many people, keeping the thermostat set at sixty degrees is downright cold. I took a lot of kidding about this. Kenny gave me a nickname that other patients picked up and used regularly. I didn't mind, because I thought it was funny and fitting. I was the Snowman. It was ironic, because "snow" also refers to drugs. Amazing irony or cosmic black humor? I don't want to guess.

As an in-patient, you're preoccupied with therapy and the "little things" that aren't so little any more. You have less time to think beyond yourself. In the transitional phase of life at Rebound, you have much more time to think, to reflect, to strengthen the part of your mind that considers abstract and philosophical ideas. This type of personal mental rehabilitation, relearning how to think by and for yourself, may be the most important part of the entire process.

One of the most significant things that happened to me during this part of my life came about as the result of a random event. I still needed a little help in putting on my coat. One cold day, I stopped a stranger and asked if he would help me put my coat on. He did, I thanked him, and he went on his way. He was just doing someone a simple favor. It was no big deal to him. But that small act made me realize that I could be accepted in the community by the world outside Rebound. It was a big deal to me.

This independent thinking probably helped me make the decision to stay in the transitional program at Rebound, although I had the opportunity to leave in August 1991. My decision was not based on fear or wanting others to do things for me. I wanted to stay to receive more therapy so I could be as healthy as possible, physically and mentally, when it came time for me to leave. And I wanted to stay to attend Longview College for a semester. Coach Shelling had always driven a famous quote into my head that Vince Lombardi made famous: "Be the best you can be."

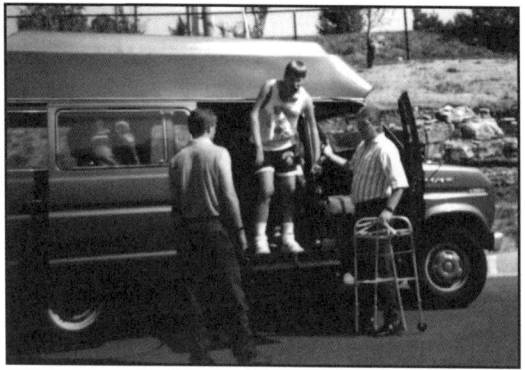
Coming home from college. Randy Leighton and Kevin Birch watching.

Longview College in Lee Summit, Missouri, just south of Kansas City, had a special program in cooperation with Rebound designed for people with learning disabilities. Project Able concentrated on preparing you for the

Mary Ellen Jenison, director of Project Able.

end of your stay at Rebound. It was the last step before you walked back into a life of your own. Those of us who made it to Project Able were driven to class four days each week. Getting out and away from the familiar settings of Rebound and simply traveling back and forth to a college setting this way made me feel more a part of the outside world. I'll always be thankful to Mary Ellen Jenison, the director of Project Able. She is a remarkably patient, caring, and inspiring individual. She used to help me with my homework and always seemed to make time for me. I'll always be thankful for her help and guidance.

Along with traditional education came social learning. We attended group functions, such as outings to watch Kansas City Royals baseball games. That was an education in itself! Everyone likes to "people watch," but for myself and others at Rebound, this was a big dose of seeing how other people interact with each other on a grand scale, from ordinary conversation to heated differences of opinion, to finding their way around in a relatively unfamiliar setting.

And I thought it was just for fun!

The emphasis at Longview was on learning, and I welcomed it. No goofing off this time around. I wanted to make the most of this renewed educational opportunity. It was at Longview that I became aware that I would be able to continue learning at advanced levels. I had always been good in math and found I could understand beginning algebra without difficulty. I still couldn't read as well as I wanted to, but I never missed a class. I listened and memorized. I was a bit of a teacher's pet, an image I would have laughed at a couple of years earlier. I was a good example for other students, who helped me to take notes, since writing was still physically difficult for me.

I concentrated. I studied. I did it. I got straight A's.

I left Project Able feeling better about myself than I had in a very long time. I had relearned the routines of daily living, deepened my appreciation and understanding of relating to other people, and reaffirmed my ability to learn.

I left Rebound on April 10, 1992, exactly two and a half years after my accident. I had to be taken in. I walked out. I couldn't go to the bathroom by myself when I went there. I left knowing I could do almost anything for myself, by myself. I began the program as a humbled, crippled kid. I ended it as a modestly proud, healed young man.

But the biggest accomplishment I made in rehabilitation had nothing to do with any of this. It was the biggest thing that ever happened in my life. It provided an understanding of how and why my life had been such a roller coaster ride. And most importantly, it gave me a framework for both the immediate future and for the rest of my life. It was a discovery I never expected to make.

INTERLUDE

Reflections and a New Outlook

Do you believe in precognitive dreams? They're usually vivid dreams, easily remembered, and likely to be dismissed as "just a dream" by most people. I had one, and it did come true.

I dreamt about the car crash that put me into the coma.

It was a dramatic dream that has always stayed with me. I still remember the date I had it: April 20, 1989. Although I don't remember all of the details precisely, I do remember dreaming I was badly injured in a terrible automobile accident. I had the clear impression I had become an example for the world.

As frightening as it was, I brushed it off as only a bad dream, a drama created by my subconscious. I thought it couldn't be anything more than a morality play, a stupid dream with a Sunday school message to be a good little boy instead of a cool sports dude. I never for a moment thought this dream might be a warning or, at the very least, a plea from another part of me struggling to say, "Hey! You're headed for a crash!" either literally or figuratively.

Whether you interpret them as messages from God or from an inner part of yourself, such dreams are important and should not be disregarded. I believe this dream was such a message, and I'll always regret ignoring it.

But why should I have paid any attention to it? Before the accident, everything was now. The future was the date of the next football game. My personal future was waiting in some untouchable void. It was a future that could only be positive and bright.

Precognition was always a part of my life. Whether a natural sense lost for some unknown reason or a more direct message from God, I'm amazed at how many clues I'd had that something big was going to happen in my life soon after I got the clues.

A couple of weeks before the accident, for example, I asked Mom, "Do I have good hospitalization insurance?" She was surprised and wondered why I was asking. I spoke from the heart: "I don't think I'm going to live to be very old.... I don't think I'm going to see my twenty-first birthday." I had not been brooding; something inside seemed to prompt me at random to think like that.

Although I'm still alive and kicking and hope to be for a long time, I did not, in fact, see my twenty-first birthday. I turned twenty-one in the hospital in a pretty murky mental state.

I don't remember the day of the accident, but Mom remembers another unusual occurrence that morning. True to form, I was in a hurry, trying to avoid being late for work. I dashed out of the house, jumped into my car, revved it up, and pulled out of the driveway. Then, although I knew it might make me late, I pulled back into the driveway, jumped out, ran back into the house, gave Mom a big hug and a kiss, and said, "I love you, Mom. You're the greatest!"

Usually, I'd just hop in the car and go. But that day, something, some cue from deep inside, urged me to take the extra minute to run back inside to tell Mom I loved her. Whatever it was that led me to break my routine, I'm glad it happened. Those were the last words she heard me say for over a year. While I was in rehabilitation, I had time to think and to ask myself serious questions. When all you can do is lie in bed for long periods of time, you have no choice but to think. Although I was determined to walk again and was motivated enough to flirt, the extent of my injuries and the sense of loss I felt combined at times to make me think about the unthinkable: suicide.

There were times when I was in the hospital I really wanted to die. I did not realize how precious life is. I relived my sports victories over and over again in my mind, and I became depressed when I realized that it would never be that way again. My old way of life—the parties, drugs, sports, and women—was ingrained. My desire for that life did not end quickly. When physical gratification is reinforced over and over, it becomes addictive—very much like using drugs.

The friendships I started to develop with other Rebound patients became important to me. I was touched every day by the caring of Rebound staff members who wanted to help me grow stronger. I was—perhaps for the first time—learning the value of the important things in life. I knew I would go to hell if I killed myself. I had never been motivated by fear before, but things were different now. I accepted the fact I wasn't such a hotshot less reluctantly than I would have earlier in my life. It's not difficult to do when you realize your body is literally bent out of shape.

But I could not ignore the support and love of my family, especially my mother. I was very much aware of what killing myself would do to them. None of the people closest to me ever lost faith. No one believed I would not come out of the coma. I knew if I killed myself, these people would not only be deeply hurt but would feel they had failed in some way. I could never accept failure for myself, so how could I do something that would cause those who loved me to feel they had failed?

It was, and is, the easy way out. If you look into the mirror, you will always find the answers to your problems staring right back at you. One of the things I thought about at Rebound was knowing how it felt to be disabled. In these days of being politically correct, let's use the right word: disabled not challenged. Challenges can be met. The career I wanted for myself had been wiped out. I was disabled. At times, I was sad and angry thinking about it. But I managed to accept my situation by consistently thinking, "How do I cope with this? What do I need to do to keep going?"

Others can empathize all they want in trying to imagine what it feels like to be disabled. But unless it happens to you, you can never fully understand it. I gained a real appreciation of those who can't do for themselves, because for a while I was one of them.

You never think to yourself, "So this is what it's like." Your attitude gradually changes until, for example, seeing someone in a wheelchair evokes no reaction whatsoever. That person is just part of the picture and not necessarily a person who needs a special accommodation.

One victory I took great pride in during rehabilitation was learning to be left-handed. My right hand was injured so much that I cannot use my fingers normally. My left hand, although it had been injured too, was more flexible. So on the recommendation of doctors, I became left-handed.

The problem was that my mind was right-handed. I had lived twenty years as a right-handed person. It seemed unnatural to do things with my left hand. Many, many times I started to do something with my right hand and then I would remember, "Oh, yeah, I gotta do this with my other hand." Frustrating, aggravating, sometimes comical, I slowly learned to make my left hand the dominant one. Today, whenever someone who doesn't know how this came to be kids me about being left-handed, I like to zap them back by saying, "Only left-handed people are in their right mind!"

Spend an hour sometime trying to use the hand you don't usually use. Forget writing—just try dressing yourself, tying your shoes, combing your hair, and even eating with the other hand. You'll gain an understanding of this problem very quickly and, in doing so, personally share one of the challenges I faced.

■ ■ ■ ■ ■

When I began learning again how to walk up and down stairs without using a handrail, I realized again how much of life we take for granted. At first I thought, "This must sound really stupid to most people." But I remembered how I used to go up and down the bleachers at different sporting events in high school. Bleachers don't have handrails except on the outside supports. If you have trouble moving or walking normally, lack of physical support can be both frightening and dangerous to you and to others. I felt a great sense of accomplishment when I was able to walk up and down steps without needing a handrail. It was as if I had regained a part of my former life—certainly a reason for at least a small celebration. When I was "officially" out of rehab and back home, one of the most unexpected and unusual situations I encountered was seeing my friends for the first time in many months. Brad Hansen, a football player and all-sports star athlete from my high

Standing in front of my trophy case holding the ball I hit a grand slam home run with against Missouri Valley.

school's arch rival Missouri Valley High school, even came to visit me. We had been extremely competitive, so I was surprised when he said to me, "If anyone could have come back, you could." His respect for me had extended beyond the playing field.

Many friends had come to see me right after the accident before I left the hospital in Omaha when I was in very bad shape. Most were shocked when they first saw me walking and talking. I was somewhat uncomfortable at this type of reception, but I knew their reactions were just part of the changes accompanying what I could rightfully call a rebirth, a new life. Some friends were afraid to approach me, probably because they didn't know what to expect. Some would come close and ask, "Do you remember me?"

This made me angry. I wanted to shout back at them, "Why wouldn't I remember you?" I realized, however, they knew I had sustained head injuries, undergone more than two years of therapy, and had no real news about me for months. I assume some must have felt bad because they had not visited me after I left the hospital in Omaha. I understood this—they had their own lives to live. And I was three hours away in Missouri. Friends are not always as close as family and that's okay.

One thing that does bother me is my lack of recollection for certain events. It always hurts me when someone asks, "Do you remember when...?" about a particular event or shared time in the past, and I have to answer, "No, I'm sorry, I don't remember."

■ ■ ■ ■ ■

Near the end of my stay at Rebound, I felt very good about myself and all of my personal accomplishments. This was not an attitude of conceit, but rather was part of the realization this part of my life was nearing an end. It was then I began to realize the things important to me before the accident were no longer important. I realized, for example, that I had come to really enjoy learning.

And yet, these changes did not seem dramatic to me. They were natural, almost logical results of rehabilitation and having had time to think. I discovered things about myself I never expected to find.

Discovery

As a youngster growing up in Iowa, my religious life was probably like that of many other kids. I went to Sunday school and attended church with my family. When you're a kid, you do it because it's expected of you and because you really have no choice.

When I became a teenager, my beliefs stayed the same but grew less intense and not as important. It wasn't "cool" to be active in religious activities. Mom tried to maintain my involvement with our faith but respected my right to make my own decisions. Unfortunately, at that time, faith was no match for sports, drugs, and sex. Any church services or functions I attended were done more for the sake of appearance than anything else.

It may sound contradictory, but although I was very self-centered before the accident that put me into the coma, I've always supported the so-called underdogs in life. In particular, I remember a short, black student in high school. He received a fair amount of taunting and teasing from other students on a regular basis. Keep in mind, there weren't many black students in small, rural Iowa high schools at the time. I didn't know him personally, and I didn't know whether or not there was any racial prejudice involved in his being teased, but it annoyed me. One day, as several students were harassing him, I stepped in and said, "Anyone who wants to hassle him has to deal with me first." Everyone backed off.

I wasn't trying to impress anyone. I just felt he was being treated unfairly, and I wanted to straighten the situation out.

At Rebound, I began to appreciate the fact that, in spite of my problems, there were others who were in worse condition than I was. I did not especially pity them, but I felt for them. I went out of my way to help them if they needed and wanted it. I helped others more often than I realized at the time. Without knowing it, I was learning to enjoy being in service to others, and I received a great deal of satisfaction from it.

Enter the Junk Food Man, also known as Bob Zerr. He was the spiritual counselor at Rebound, and although Bob wasn't the chaplain, he did a chaplain's service, helping to meet the religious needs of all the patients there. He took us to the chapel, conducted services himself once in awhile, and could rightfully be called Rebound's religious ombudsman.

Bob had a wonderful personality. He smiled a lot and was very reassuring to everyone. Although he never passed up an opportunity to try to persuade you to attend services or visit the chapel, he never leaned on you. His suggestions to beef up your spiritual life were never threatening or heavy-handed.

I liked Bob a lot—at first because he supplied me with snacks I wasn't supposed to have. That's how he got the nickname Junk Food Man. I'm sure Rebound would not have been happy to learn how much candy and sweet stuff he provided for me.

Bob was always asking me to go to the chapel. And I always said no. I had no interest in hearing someone preach.

Then one day, I asked Bob to take me to the chapel.

He laughed, thinking I was making a joke of some kind. But I wasn't. Make no mistake: I did not have some kind of dramatic revelation, some blinding flash of realization that said I must be born again. It wasn't a desperate move, a quick decision. It was simply the right thing to do.

I had nowhere else to go but up. I didn't like the position I was in and was willing to do anything to get out of it. I was still determined to walk and to lead a normal life again someday, but I was tired. I knew it was God who had pushed away my thoughts of suicide. And I had a feeling I had been spared from death in both accidents for a reason other than extreme luck.

Bob was delighted. He took me to the chapel where he read from the Bible. I let myself open up and felt a great sense of calm and satisfaction. Realizing I was still recuperating and in therapy, Bob frequently asked me, "Do you want to stop now?" But I felt so good, I answered, "No," every time. We read for three and a half hours.

I went to the chapel every chance I could after that. I never grew tired of hearing someone read from the Bible and later of reading it myself. I found answers to questions I had thought about many times at Rebound. I understood what had happened to me and why. I discovered that being born again means being figuratively reborn for yourself, as well as for God.

Two things became clear soon after I started to go to the chapel regularly. I knew God had spared my life in the first car crash because he was trying to teach me a lesson, to give me a second chance. I am sure He was warning me. It was a stiff warning, but at the time, it was the only type of language I understood…and I still didn't listen! I know He's forgiven me, but I still have moments from time to time when I feel deep regret for not listening earlier.

It also became clear God had a purpose for me going through what I did. I wasn't sure at the time what it was, but today I am: God saved me so I could help others.

The enjoyment of helping others at Rebound while being severely challenged myself laid the groundwork to make my decision to rediscover God more natural and easy. I went from virtually no religion to too much religion. I wanted to spread the word to everybody. I became a pest. Thanks to Bob's guidance and the patience I learned as a result of my extended recuperation, I learned to keep my passion for preaching under control.

I still get so excited sometimes I have to remind myself God speaks to each person only at the speed at which they can hear. I continue to strive for balance today.

Before my second accident, I went to church occasionally just to see my friends and please my mother. Now I go every Sunday for the right reasons: to worship God and to thank Him for all He has done for me. I know God guided the hands of all the doctors who operated on me and gave me the strength to pull through fourteen surgeries. If I ever start feeling down, all I have to do is to watch some of the videotape made of me just before I began rehabilitation. I look terrible and fairly hopeless. Seeing it reminds me how powerful the Lord is. I wouldn't be anywhere without Him.

Old habits really do die hard. From time to time, I have flashes of the "old" Scott trying to come through, to return to the lifestyle that almost destroyed me. But the "new" Scott wants to leave him dead and buried. I hate the devil with a passion.

One of the things I've done to mark the transition from my druggie days to now is to change my name. I was Scott Krumwiede; now I'm Scott McPhillips. McPhillips is my father's name. He died when I was quite young. Everyone in my family says he was strong-willed and I look and act like him. Changing my name signifies a new start, as well as going back to my roots. And getting back to your roots means getting back to God.

And besides, I like the nickname "Mac."

■ ■ ■ ■ ■

For the longest time, I wondered why I had to go through everything I did as a result of the second car crash. I know now it was not a punishment. It was a random act, caused by my stupidity. God felt bad about it, too. He doesn't want to see us hurt ourselves. Yes, God has control over everything. But he gave us free will and keeps His hands off when we make a decision that results in pain. If he didn't, it wouldn't really be free will. Thankfully, His love and healing power gives us the way to correct our mistakes.

And for some of us who need it, He gives a second chance at life, too.

■ ■ ■ ■ ■

I've kept a personal journal for a long time. I started it during rehabilitation, having other people, especially my mother, write down my thoughts for me. In looking over the notes I made at the beginning of 1992, I'm reminded of the determination that has always been such a strong part of my life. I still feel today the way I did then when I wrote, "I believe deep in my heart that I can become whatever I really set my mind to. I can accomplish anything."

I want to coach someday. As a matter of fact, I want to coach a state championship. This isn't a way of trying to recapture past personal glories. Thanks to the Lord, I know I'm on a mission to teach all I know to youths so they will not have any of the pitfalls I had.

Coaching will have to have to wait for a little while, though. Right now, I want to tell my story to as many people as possible. That's why I wrote this book. That's why I speak to groups whenever I can.

The message is simple: Don't do drugs.

But it's getting harder and harder to get the message across. "Just say no" is a great idea but it's too simplistic. Nothing beats experience, and Lord knows, I've had that! No one should have to go through what I did.

I don't want to preach. I want to tell my story. People listen to stories and can learn from them. Hellfire, brimstone, and damnation only work on people who are already frightened. I hope if young people can identify with me, they might vicariously share even a little of my experience and get the message. It's a lot easier to learn from seeing someone else burn their fingers on a hot stove than to do it yourself.

It makes me feel really good when I know people hear what I'm saying. I spoke to a group of head-injured patients and their families at St. Joseph's Hospital in Omaha while I was completing my rehabilitation. I could see hope in their eyes when I told them I had been in worse condition than they were then. I was thrilled to be an inspiration to them.

Following some high school presentations, I've had one or two students come up to talk with me following my speech. I remember one girl who was crying as she approached. I said to her, "Hey, stop crying. This isn't a sad occasion. This is a happy occasion. I can talk and walk, and you heard what I said." She was sorry for what I had gone through and it moved her deeply. I knew my message was indeed being heard.

I spend a lot of time now talking to people everywhere about God and his message. The thank you notes and letters I've received are some of my greatest rewards. I spoke at Beveridge Junior High School and Benson High school in Omaha, Nebraska, and got a very special letter. I was told some of the Benson students had been moved to tears. In addition, the following thoughts were expressed:

> Your message is very personal and very painful. The issue of drunk driving or driving under the influence of any drugs is current and sometimes tragic. Because your message is so personal, it really does have power. The format of starting with the "healthy" video and having your mother talk while the rehabilitation film plays silently in the background is very effective. Young people tend to forget that their actions do affect other people. When you follow this and start talking about the emotional pain (losing your friend and your life as you knew it), and the physical pain, it becomes phenomenally powerful. I believe you are right Scott. You have had 2 strikes but you're not going to strike out. You are going to the TOP! Thank you so much.

Another note had these encouraging thoughts:

> I just wanted to let you know that I enjoyed visiting with you on Saturday. It was a most interesting story that you have to tell, as for the difficulties and adjustments that you had to adjust to. You are truly an amazing young man to have the positive attitude you do. Keep up the good attitude and the Lord will *guide* you.

I participated in a mini-course day at the Logan-Magnolia Community School District in Logan, Iowa, which was very well received; I've been invited to participate in the next one. I've spoken to young people at shopping malls, where on more than one occasion, I've been told that people have rediscovered their relationship with God after hearing my story. This is what it takes for me to feel good about my life now. What a contrast with how I used to try to make myself feel good.

■ ■ ■ ■ ■

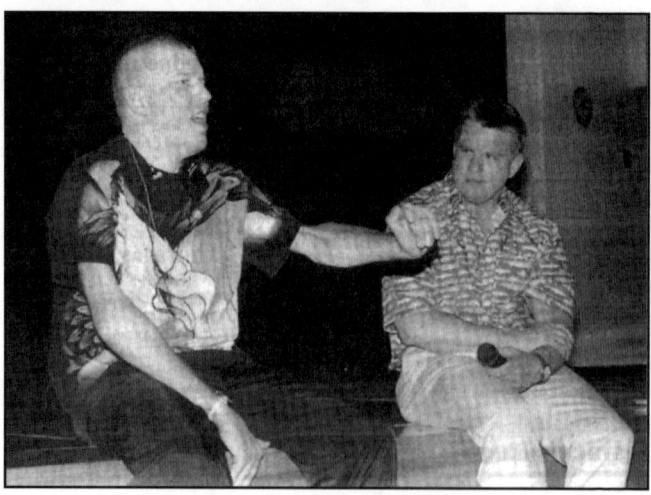

Coach Gaylord Schelling and I talking to the Atlantic kids.

Another high point for me is a newspaper article about me and my high school coach—and friend—Gaylord Schelling. The article by Colleen Mullen of the Atlantic *News-Telegraph* (Iowa) (April 4, 1997) details my past life and the accident, and how this can make students think about what the consequences may be of abusing alcohol and drugs.

> ...But they also see "his [Scott's] will to live, his will to win. He refused to die at that time [of the accident]," Schelling added. "...Often times it's easy for someone to give up. People have to see in life, if you have a will, you can make it."
>
> Some people may feel sorry for what happened to him, but Scott does not feel sorry for himself. He believes it is not too late to influence others, make a difference in others' lives, and live an enriched, full life in the eyes of God.
>
> ...Things people take for granted each day, was something Scott was challenged with. But he didn't give up. Schelling can vouch for that.
>
> "Right now, he's a good example to others," he said.
>
> He's someone who values each breath he takes, each step he is able to walk.

Each day he has to face what happened on that grim day.

Each day he works to make amends with God, and asks for his forgiveness.

Gaylord Schelling always kept up with my rehabilitation and recovery, even after he left Tri-Center High School to take a coaching job in Atlantic, Iowa. I was honored when he asked me to talk to his team the night of their eighth game, following seven straight losses, in October 1991. I was a little apprehensive at the thought of speaking for my former coach in a setting that would bring together the good times that had been so important to me and the reality that I had caused my own dreams to be shattered.

I wrote the speech without much trouble. Because of my injuries, I could not speak well enough then to deliver the talk. Even today, sometimes it's physically difficult for me to speak. I asked Bryan White to deliver my speech. Bryan was a high school classmate I always thought of as a real goody-two-shoes. Today, he's one of my closest friends.

This is what I wrote and what Bryan said:

> Coach Schelling has asked me to say a few words to you.
>
> What do I think it takes to win? I strongly believe it takes hard work and heart in wanting something more than you have ever wanted something before.
>
> Say you are behind in the fourth quarter—somehow, some way, you will find a way to win. I was never supposed to walk but I would not believe that. Don't you believe it when people say you are not supposed to win. Find a way to win, somehow, some way.
>
> If you have any belief in Coach Schelling, you will give the game your all. You have to give the game your all. I did not realize how lucky I was until I lost it; now I'm having to give it my all just to try to be normal.
>
> Remember, you have to believe in yourself and others will learn to believe in you. If you believe you are defeated, you are

defeated. So believe you are a winner and come back after the game a winner. Now, go fight, and do it for yourself. The one you really have to please is yourself.

My biggest words of wisdom are the ones I live by every day: persistence overcomes resistance. That's how I've come as far as I have. My doctor said I would never walk, but I would not believe him. It all comes down to what you believe in your heart. If you believe you are always going to come out a winner, you will win. It all comes from the heart.

I knew many people who were more talented than I was, but I would not accept defeat at their hands. I would give anything to be able to do it all over again, but now you have to do it for me.

I am with you all the way.

Coach Schelling's team beat Glenwood 33–32 that day—Atlantic's only win of the season.

■ ■ ■ ■ ■

And I am with *you* all the way, too. Thank you for reading my story. May God bless you.

AFTERWORD

Scott McPhillips From the Eyes of Others

FROM SCOTT'S MOM

Life is full of good times and challenges. God never gives us more than we can handle, but raising Scott made me wonder more than once!

Scott was a very strong willed little boy who always wanted to be as big as his older brother. He played very hard and always strived to be the best.

His accomplishments in sports brought much happiness to me. All the way from PeeWee baseball to the Iowa State Tournament, I loved to sit behind the fence and watch him pitch. To watch him outjump 6'5" basketball players or catch the winning touchdown in football made me proud to be known as "Scott's mom." But, watching Scott overcome the injuries and trauma of his head injury by far exceeded any previous mother to son admiration.

When Scott came home from Rebound, April 10, 1992, exactly 2½ years after his accident, I took him to Immanuel Hospital for additional therapy. When tested for speech accuracy, he had an 11% intelligible factor. They taped a conversation and another therapist wrote down what was understandable.

When Scott started Iowa Western Community College in the fall of 1992, he was still at the same intelligible factor. They gave him a private room, since no one could share a room at 60 degrees. Scott's temperature control in his brain was damaged and he was always hot. The only way we could ride in comfort was if he wore shorts and a tank top and I wore a sweatshirt and winter coat. Of course when we stopped anywhere, accusing eyes said, "You don't even put a coat on this disabled kid?"

Another reason for staying alone was sleep patterns. Sometimes he would be up most of the night with sleeplessness. Studying took total concentration. We got tapes from the visually impaired on the subjects he took. I'll never forget one class we couldn't get tapes for. I worried over what we could do. They said it would take four months to tape and by that time the class would be over. One night coming home from work while driving, I talked to God. While asking God what can I do, a voice said to me "Tape it yourself." How easy answers can be sometimes. The only request Scott made was that someone else do the taping since he heard mom's voice so much.

The college let us remodel his dorm key. A rod was welded onto the key and a hole through the rod and put on a necklace to go around his neck. His hands were not able to get keys out of his pocket.

Life became a new ritual. Scott had a refrigerator in his dorm room in which he kept his doughnuts and milk for breakfast and snacks for lunch. I got off work at 3:30 p.m., picked up Scott to go out for dinner, talked over the goodness and problems of the day, helped with any homework left to do, and anything else that needed to be done. His hands were good enough to take care of his body needs, but not to do everything that needed to be done (clean room, washing clothes—woman's stuff). I wanted to make his stay at college as easy as possible. Scott could have gone to the college cafeteria to eat, but that was across campus. I was afraid he would be too tired after a long day and would go hungry rather than go to the cafeteria. Scott's eating habits were still not the best at this time. Due to the head injury when trying to eat, his hands would shake and the food would fall off the fork before getting to his mouth.

Most of the kids at IWCC were really helpful and kind—being 18 years old, taking the patience and time to listen to a young man with an 11% intelligible factor who walked with an unsteady gait. After 3 months at IWCC, Scott's intelligible factor increased dramatically because he talked so much and was trying harder than ever to make himself understood. With all those pretty girls around, he wanted them to know what he was saying. Same old charmer Scott.

There was always the worry during the winter months—icy sidewalks—but mostly his inability to feel cold. One day when it was -60 degrees wind chill factor, he walked all the way across campus with just a t-shirt and sweatpants on. He very seldom wore a coat as it was too hard to get on, he got too hot when he got into a building, and it was too hard to carry when he took it off.

Scott really enjoyed his stay at Iowa Western. He greatly advanced both physically and spiritually. I have to believe he was a bit favored by most. He had many who helped him. At the top of the list was Mike Wulbecker who helped him physically in the weight room, emotionally to deal with everyday situations, and to continue his spiritual walk with God. He was as a father to Scott, listening, disciplining as necessary, and being the friend he needed. David Hufford helped with his drinking problem, taking him to AA, and became a good friend. Being Scott, not afraid to talk to anyone, the Dean of IWCC, Robert Franzese, did not escape Scott on a daily basis.

As Scott states, "I have to mention the woman who put up with a lot of my crap, Jeanne Snyder. Jeanne helped me with reading and writing and my temper. I'm sure I tried her patience as much as she tried mine. I loved her and she appreciated and loved me. She has done extensive study on head injuries since I've left and she says it really helped her understand why I was the way I was. Iowa Western was just the place I needed to be. The people were very caring and loving. I have been back since I graduated, and it is still a great school. They have no one like I was—lucky for them."

Another challenge—Scott wanted to start driving again. Trying to give Scott a new outlook on life, we looked for and bought a new car in July 1993. Little did I know when we bought this red 1993 Pontiac Sunbird with black interior, fancy rim wheels, great radio system, cassette player, spoiler, etc. that he would actually get a license soon. It was like a catalyst and in November 1993 I finally gave in and said he could take the test for a permit to learn to drive. Without even reading or preparing for the driver's test, he passed with flying colors. The license bureau read the questions and answers for him and he responded with the answer. At this point it was still difficult to read. The muscles in his eyes were better, but still not focusing right to read.

Now we had a new challenge. At least Scott didn't want to drive on icy roads, so there was a little reprieve. In May 1994, he wanted to take the driving test to get his license. I wanted him to wait. When he was driving out of town one night, I told him to slow down, that he was going too fast. He said he wasn't, that the speed limit was 40 MPH. I said 35. He said if I'm right will you let me try for my license. I said yes because I knew I was right. I don't know when they changed the limit, but an agreement is an agreement.

The first time he failed and the examiner said she could have passed him, but she wanted him to have more driving practice. She felt he would not stay on the back roads for awhile, but would drive right in downtown Omaha immediately. I said, "Thank you." She had good perception. We drove and drove for a week and went back for retesting. They drove for a half hour during rush hour traffic on the main streets. He came back in with the biggest grin and she said he had points to spare. Lost the red car with less than 12,000 miles on it. Those wheels never stop now, 90,000 and continuing. Independence has never meant so much to Scott as well as to mom.

Today, Scott and I love to talk to school children, or anyone that will listen. The dead silence and respect that is shown, indeed reflects that our message is being heard. "Drugs are a lie, Jesus is the truth." Starting with a healthy video, highlights of a sports jock, to the Rebound video, the virtually hopeless young man through his next 26 months of recovery, played in silence while we talk. I'll always wish I would have had more "tough love" while Scott was growing up and maybe we could have eliminated some of the pitfalls. We truly hope that people can learn for us instead of going through the trials and tribulations we have had to face.

I have a real admiration for my son, the challenges he has faced, and his love and commitment to God. He never ceased to amaze me with the play to win the game, but now the greatest game of all, "The Game of Life." I am honored to be know as "Scott's mom."

FROM DAVID HUFFORD

I first met Scott McPhillips when he was a student at Iowa Western Community College sometime in 1993, and have remained his friend until this day. He was never a student of mine, but never has a person been more a student of mine. My first impression of Scott—I blush to admit it—was being not a little frightened of him. I did not know Scott as he was, as I had heard he was. I had heard he had been a fine student of great promise, and an excellent, a great, athlete. I had heard he had gone away to college, and had been in a terrible accident. That was all I knew. I had no particular expectations. And since Scott had never been in any of my classes, I had had no occasion to talk to him.

I probably would not have talked to him. Scott presented a rather fearful aspect. It was not just the fact that some miracle of modern medicine had pieced together the man who I saw, but that Scott was also frightening of aspect, with a loud, but unsteady voice, and an intense demeanor.

When at last I chanced to meet him—he had come to the English Department Office to see someone else—he stopped to talk to me. I was uncertain how to proceed—Scott's enunciation becomes clear enough when you are familiar with it—but I suddenly felt a need to communicate. And I as Communication teacher, was uncertain how to proceed. The opening came on two or three points of truth: we both insisted on the truth—hard line truth. We both insisted on fearlessly stating and expounding our religious convictions and spiritual insights, and we both had some kind of problem with alcohol. I am an alcoholic. Scott needed to talk to someone about things which also apparently included just needing to speak freely and truthfully, to talk about his deepening belief, and to talk about problems of his medical and physical condition, his past, his wreck, his purportedly previous drinking that had led to his personal disaster.

All these things he told me in painfully slow and broken sentences. When he stopped at some point, I was immediately all over him: I recall my first sentence to a man who had frightfully suffered more than most of us will know: "Clean the wax out of your ears."

What I believe I was hearing at that point is what admitted and recovering alcoholics refer to as *denial*. Scott had been through much in his physical and mental recovery, but there was still much churning around in him of an emotional and spiritual nature.

Later it would come out always in terms of how much Jesus Christ had done for him, the power of which Scott was possessed to do the will of God, as of one powerfully converted by the most astonishing of circumstances; for that is actually what the situation was. But I felt there were issues which Scott was not dealing with, sometimes admitting, but not totally acknowledging.

But to tell such a person to clean the wax out of his ears was a harsh beginning. But it got his attention—not because I was out to get his attention, but that I had one thing to offer him: I had suffered different things but for the same reason: the bottle. And I had also done damage while drunk. And I had to admit not my power but my powerlessness, and turn my will and life over to God. I drank not because of some madman's insane desire for alcohol, but why all of us do: that one drink will trigger an obsession that will not let us stop. And we drink to fill some interior black hole that nothing will fill.

Scott was trying to fill the black hole with the right stuff without going through the process of getting back out of where he had gotten. Religion, positive thinking, education, hard work—all are fine things, but what some of us need is an inside job.

Scott was arrested by my candor, and thereafter we could always talk openly about everything. (Eventually this entailed going to AA meetings.) My office became a more exciting place of dialogue than most classrooms. We could seek the truth in utter disagreement while deeply respecting the spoken spirituality we were both capable of stating. Nevertheless it was not until after Scott could say "I killed a man," and "I drove after I lined up ten shots of Jack Daniels," that the blockade was cleared.

Scott began to pull away from organized recovery groups, for his spiritual bent was more in the direction of the open declaration of what Jesus Christ had done for him. But I think the exchange of his ideas with others in recovery was valuable for all of them.

It is clear that Scott has a message that is born of suffering and the positive lessons that one can turn such an experience into. Scott goes many directions: I will try to get him to keep it simple, as in Christ's words. "Fear not; only believe." Both of us are similar in belief: both deriving from Lutheranism, both spiritual mavericks.

Through our various sufferings, we learn to love, to seek justice, and to forgive. It would be wrong to suggest that Scott and I have been these great spiritual geniuses: we are buddies who became friends. We have talked as much about women and sex as about God and recovery. We are men.

But Scott has helped me become more the kind of man I also need to be: one more like him: more willing to witness, more willing to speak the nearest good thing and to do the first best thing. Scott has taught me to be unafraid to speak and do my convictions as fearlessly as he does.

FROM DEAN ROBERT FRANZESE

I first met Scott in the fall term of 1992. This was the first time that I would ever set eyes on Scott. I must admit, I was startled by his condition, which I knew nothing about at that time. Scott walked very slowly and cautiously, and his speech was nearly unintelligible for me. I first encountered Scott as he was walking into a psychology course taught by Terry Miller. Scott approached Terry and proceeded to attempt to explain to him his needs, which quickly became apparent. Scott was going to need special attention and services, which the College has provided to its students throughout its history. During that first encounter with Mr. Miller and me, Scott told us of his automobile accident that was responsible for his disabilities. It was a very sad story, and it was extremely difficult to understand Scott. His speech was slurred, and the words spoken were indistinguishable from one another.

To state that Scott was a "unique" individual would be a major understatement. He continued for at least a full semester to walk very slowly, and to speak in an unclear manner. But by the spring term, Scott had begun to walk with more confidence, and his speech improved markedly, although he was still difficult to understand. His turnaround appeared to have a lot to do with Mike Wulbecker, who at that time was the athletic director and professor of physical education. Mr. Wulbecker took Scott under his wings, and worked with him daily, on his speech and on his physical condition. As a result, Scott became stronger and more confident. He also began to become more appreciated by his student peers. With his increasing self confidence, Scott's grades also improved, and Scott made the great strides needed to proceed down the path toward graduation.

As Scott assimilated more into Iowa Western, he became quite the admirer of the coed population (something tells me that this had always been an interest of Scott's). He was seen frequently with women—even if they did not invite him into their conversations or where they were seated. But Scott was making progress with every day: he spoke more clearly, and carried himself with pride and positive demeanor. In one year, Scott became a "new man," and during this period, this formerly perplexed young man found faith, again through the efforts of Mike Wulbecker.

Scott graduating from Iowa Western Community College, August 1, 1994.

For me, the defining point in my experience with Scott was when he graduated from Iowa Western during the summer of 1994. To see him walk across the stage and receive his degree was a highlight of my 23 years with the college. In all respects, Scott has changed for the better, and he continues to have goals and to grow as a man with a bright future.

FROM TODD HARRISON

I met Scott several years ago. I remember how he was so willing to talk to whoever would listen. Very shortly after that first meeting, Scott was a student in Public Speaking class. I thought to myself, Will Scott get along in this class with other students? Will he be able to get his point across in the assigned speeches? I saw Scott, in the middle of winter, walking up College Road with no coat or hat on. I had to approach him the next day to ask "why?" He simply told me he didn't need a coat or hat, and that was that. During the semester and years afterward I learned a lot about Scott. His aspirations, his beliefs, and his determination. He inspired so many people, because Scott is not a quitter.

He did well in Public Speaking, always volunteered to be first to speak, which made the other students happy. He fulfilled Speech assignments like a champ. Other students got to know Scott. They respected him and listened to his message about not giving up. I think over the years Scott and I became friends. At least, I hope so, because he has been an inspiration to me.

SPEECH

On the Rebound

Written by Bill Henjum for Scott McPhillips

Bill: You've probably read about someone who has been drunk in a car accident where a life has been lost. You've probably read about someone who's been in a coma for months. You've probably read about someone who's had to blink once for "yes" and twice for "no."

Scott: You've probably read about someone like me.

I will go back to the time when I was known as Scott Krumwiede. He was a very wild little boy. He played very hard and he's paid very hard. I'd like to share a little about me today.

In high school I was one cocky little boy. I was at the top of the world.

Bill: Scott was at the top of the world. He was an all-state athlete in football, basketball, and baseball, and had a reasonable chance of becoming a professional athlete. I'll tell you why.

In 1985 and 1986, he helped his team, the Tri-Center Trojans from Neola, Iowa, to second place finishes, runner-ups, in the state basketball and baseball tournaments, and Scott's team also made the state football play-offs.

In one football game, he caught a 65-yard reception for a touchdown and ran 55 yards for another to win the game against Griswold, 26–25. As a senior on the basketball team, he averaged 26 points and 12 rebounds a game. However....

Scott: I do not remember the greatest accomplishment of my sports career.

Bill: Scott and the Trojans were the Iowa state baseball champions in 1987.

Scott: They tell me I pitched a pretty good game. The first time at bat, I hit a home run.

Bill: For his pitching and hitting, he was named the Most Valuable Player for the tournament.

Scott: I'm sure you can understand how much it bothers me that I can't remember events going back to 1986. I can't even remember being the MVP of the state championship.

Bill: In the fall of 1987, this cocky little boy was off to Simpson College in Indianola, Iowa. He went there because he could play ball.

Scott: I went there to have fun, but it was the wrong kind of fun, and I'll tell you why in a moment.

Bill: As a freshman, Scott started on the varsity football team at free safety. He was known as the maniac.

Scott: On a Wednesday night after the fifth football game, my friend and I were out.

Bill: Boozing it up after a trip to Des Moines in his brother's new, black Eurosport.

Scott: Having what we thought was fun. And wham.

Bill: No one knows what happened exactly, but the car ended up against a guardrail. They told him that he wasn't driving.

Scott: All I can remember from that wreck is running down the railroad tracks and falling in the cinders with a broken bone sticking out of my arm.

Bill: The cops caught him, and he was helicoptered to the hospital in Des Moines.

Scott: Lucky or not, the cops never took a blood sample, but the hospital sample was .04 (dead drunk). God was trying to teach me a lesson that time, but I didn't learn, true to form.

Bill: It was a struggle to come back after the accident, but he made the varsity baseball team as a pitcher. It was tough to hit because of his broken arm, but he could still pitch.

Scott: And, boy, they wanted me to pitch. Anyone with a 94-mile-per-hour fast ball can blow them away.

Bill: That spring, while throwing batting practice, a line-drive hit right back at him; fractured his right eye socket.

Scott: Which ended my spring training trip to Florida. And boy, did I want to see those bikinis.

Then on October 10th, 1989, my body and my whole world were shattered. The car I was driving collided head-on into an oncoming vehicle, driven by my friend and my brother's best friend.

Bill: It happened on a gravel road at the crest of a hill. He was coming home from a bar, drunk, which was nothing new. As a matter of fact, his blood alcohol was .014 five hours after the wreck, which means he had been dead drunk.

Scott: And my friend—my brother's best friend—was killed. Lucky or not, I lived. I am very thankful now. The message came through that time, loud and clear.

Bill: It took ten hours of surgery to put his body back together again and save his life.

Scott: I never want anyone here to experience how it feels to know someone has died because of your stupidity. Whenever I think about it, which is often, it's like a knife stuck into my heart.

Bill: We hope you won't be that stupid, but some of you may be thinking, just like Scott was…

Scott: It will never happen to me.

Bill: But it did happen to Scott, and he's had to suffer tremendous consequences.

Scott: And suffer I have.

Bill: One day he woke up in the hospital. He didn't know where he was, what had happened, or even what year it was.

Scott: I saw two people come into the room and they gestured to each other and pointed at me. I was terrified, but I couldn't move. They came closer to the bed and said...

Bill: Don't be afraid, we won't hurt you. We want to ask you a few questions. Do you care?

Scott: Like I was really in a position to argue.

Bill: Do you know your name?

Scott: I couldn't talk, but I could mouth the words.

Bill: Great, he knows his name.

Scott: I'd been Scott all my life! What's wrong with these people?

Bill: Do you know what happened to you?

Scott: I mouthed "drug overdose." I had been taking so much of so many different drugs that I figured if I ever ended up in a hospital, that would be why. I was stupid, sick, a loser. They said...

Bill: No, you were in a serious car accident.

Scott: That explained why I couldn't move a muscle. As Doctor Spock would say, it was logical.

Bill: One more question. Do you know what year it is?

Scott: I thought to myself, these people think I'm wacko because I knew it was 1989.

Bill: July 1990.

Scott: I had been in a coma for nine months. Wow!

Bill: Nine months. An entire school year. Thirty-nine weekends. Thanksgiving, Christmas, Easter, and the Fourth of July. His twenty-first birthday. Nine months.

Scott: All I could think was, "I want my mommy."

Bill: He couldn't talk for a whole year, unable to communicate feelings or needs.

Scott: The only thing I could do was blink my eyes once for "yes" and twice for "no."

Bill: Can you imagine how frustrating it was for a twenty-one-year-old man who couldn't do anything for himself?

Scott: This was a guy who was a super-jock. I even had to have people help me to go to the bathroom. I couldn't talk for about over a year, but now I won't shut up.

Bill: Scott went through a period when he didn't want to live anymore.

Scott: I knew I'd never play ball again.

Bill: But then he began to realize how precious life is…

Scott: And understand that playing ball is not everything.

Bill: Since his accident, Scott has had fourteen surgeries, on both legs, both arms, and both hands.

Scott: I haven't had surgery on my brain, but I've always needed that.

Bill: Things that everyone else takes for granted, Scott had to learn to do all over again. Things like eating, standing by himself, taking steps, talking.

Scott: I am heavily indebted to a rehabilitation unit named Rebound, located in Kansas City. The wonderful people there worked with me over two years in therapy, sometimes creating more pain than you can imagine—

Bill: In order to make his hands, arms, and legs function again.

Scott: At Rebound, I had a best friend. His name was Kenny. We both had head injuries and had a lot of trouble talking.

Bill: Kenny'd fallen two stories off a roof.

Scott: We came up with our own lingo—we were the only two who could understand what we were saying. We could talk about the nurses and then laugh. It drove them crazy.

Let me tell you about the brace I had to wear during my recovery.

Bill: Scott had to pre-stretch his arms before surgery.

Scott: It was the most painful thing of my recovery. Like bones just before they break. But they wouldn't take the braces off. I wanted to use a few choice words.

Bill: It was a major accomplishment for Scott when he was able to put on his own socks and shoes.

Scott: They told me, if I ever walked again, it would be a miracle. Guess what? Miracles happen.

Bill: His mom tells a story.

Scott: I'll tell you how much my mother loves me. When I was at Rebound, she drove 888 miles, fifteen hours, every weekend so I could come home.

Bill: The doctors told her the more Scott sees his old surroundings, the faster he will recover, so Beverly, even though it put a tremendous strain on her...

Scott: My mom made sure I was home as much as possible.

Bill: Beverly knew how much Scott wanted to walk on his own...

Scott: And prove the doctors wrong.

Bill: One day when he was home...

Scott: She peeked out the window and watched me walk—on my own—a third of a mile to my grandparents' house. The surprise and joy on their faces was worth the effort. On that day, Mom tells me, she knew I'd be okay.

Walking at Grandpa and Grandma's house.

Bill: Scott's older brother had a big surprise for him.

Scott: This really blew me away; my brother pushed me in my wheelchair into the garage at our house, and there was this bitchin'

silver Camaro with a T-top. I said, "Cool, man, whose is that?"

He said...

Bill: "It's yours."

Scott: I said, "No really, whose is it?"

Bill: "It's yours. Really. You had this car before the wreck. You were driving your work car. This was your party car."

Scott: I couldn't remember being the baseball MVP and I couldn't remember my most prized possession, that silver Camaro.

Bill: Scott has told you a little about the physical pain, but the emotional pain was new to him.

Scott: That was what really hurt. One night when I was in college at Iowa Western, at two-thirty in the morning, some fools, two guys and a girl, were drunk coming home from the bar, and thought it would be funny to harass me.

Bill: They pounded on his dorm room door...

Scott: Scared the hell out of me...

Bill: And said, "Na-na-na." Then they took off down the hall laughing.

Scott: I opened the door and yelled, "I love you," as loud as I could.

Bill: Which at that time wasn't much.

Scott: Outside the next day, I saw the woman walking to class. I yelled, "Hey, I know it was you."

Bill: She started walking faster.

Scott: I yelled again, "You can run from me, but not from God."

Bill: That stopped her. She came back to him and said...

Scott: "I'm sorry. That was stupid of us. You don't know how bad I feel."

Bill: And he said...

Scott: It's all forgiven. We all make mistakes.

Bill: Do you know why people do the wrong thing?

Scott: Because it's easy. Doing the right thing is hard.

Bill: Scott lifts weights now and he sort of enjoys the physical pain of lifting…

Scott: But nothing can compare to the emotional suffering of being laughed at and the butt of jokes.

Bill: Scott has turned into the type of person he used to dislike.

Scott: A good student.

Bill: When he attended Longview College in Grandview, Missouri, guess what?

Scott: I got straight A's. That's pretty good for a guy with two head injuries.

Bill: They said he'd never be able to learn again. Nevertheless, Scott graduated from Iowa Western in Council Bluffs with an Associate of Arts Degree in 1994.

There are no easy answers in life. Doing the right thing can be hard.

Scott: It hasn't been easy going from who I was to who I am, but I like myself now. One step further, I love myself now. If you can't love yourself, how can you expect someone else to?

Bill: Scott never has learned the easy way.

Scott: And I believe God saved me for a reason, to help young people learn from my mistakes.

Bill: In January of 1994, he legally changed his name to Scott McPhillips.

Scott: I wanted my real daddy's name.

Bill: And now he's a new person.

Scott: So you can call me Mac; all my friends do.

Bill: I know you've heard this before, but it's true and should be repeated as often as possible.

Scott: You don't need to drink or do drugs to make friends or have fun.

Bill: The consequences are too great.

Scott: Don't let what happened to me happen to you.

Bill: Friends may come and go throughout your life…

Scott: But your family is yours forever. When you get home, give them a big hug for me.

Bill: Don't take anything for granted, not your family, not sports, not life itself, not eternity.

Scott: When I was sitting where you are now, I was really good at doing the wrong thing. Look at where it got me.

Bill: Do the right thing.

Scott: Do it today. Procrastination is the assassination of motivation. Wow, that's a mouthful, but I just like saying it.

Bill: If you can't do it alone, then talk to someone else. See a teacher, a counselor, a minister. Talk to Sco—Mac after the program. Talk to your mom and dad. Talk to a friend and go get help together.

Scott: We all make mistakes. Don't let a mistake change your life forever.

Bill: Losers let it happen!

Scott: Winners make it happen! I was a loser and lousy things happened to me. Now I'm a winner. I'm taking control and g-r-e-a-t, great things are happening.

Bill: In the coming years, we'll probably read about someone drunk in a car accident. We'll probably read about someone spending months in a coma or someone who can only blink for "yes" and "no."

Scott: I don't ever want to read about you. I almost died. You don't have to. Be careful. Be safe. God has been my strength. And God bless you all.

Give the Gift of Inspiration to Your Friends and Colleagues

CHECK YOUR LEADING BOOKSTORE OR ORDER HERE

❑ **YES**, I want _____ copies of *Superman Doesn't Live Here Anymore* at $9.95 paperback or $14.95 hardcover, plus $3 shipping per book (Iowa residents please add $.60 paperback or $.90 hardcover sales tax per book). Canadian orders must be accompanied by a postal money order in U.S. funds. Allow 15 days for delivery.

My check or money order for $_____ is enclosed.
Please charge my ❑ Visa ❑ MasterCard

Name _____

Phone _____

Organization _____

Address _____

City/State/Zip _____

Card # _____

Exp. Date_____ Signature _____

Please make your check payable and return to:
Mac on the Attack for Jesus
28535 Coldwater Avenue
Honey Creek, IA 51542

Call your credit card order to: (712) 545-3003
Fax: (402) 572-4454
E-mail: bkrumwiede@aol.com